THE TEARS OF PAN

Michael Finelli

 FriesenPress

One Printers Way
Altona, MB R0G 0B0
Canada

www.friesenpress.com

ISBN
978-1-03-830246-5 (Hardcover)
978-1-03-830245-8 (Paperback)
978-1-03-830247-2 (eBook)

1. POETRY, SUBJECTS & THEMES, DEATH, GRIEF, LOSS

Distributed to the trade by The Ingram Book Company

Table of Contents

Foreword

When shall the hopes of my dreams belay the depths of my sorrow?

Dear Reader,

The crucible of life creates art. Inspiration for this work was taken from many divergent rivers, all leading to the sea of creativity. Themes of darkness, depression, loneliness, self-loathing, mythology, religion, and love were woven with cathartic warp and weft into a tapestry named the human condition.

The road of existence is scarcely an easy one to traverse, even at the best of times. Sorrowful darts seem to always be shot by fate's cruel bow at the most inopportune moments, an ever-waiting highwayman. The star-kissed ocean of dreams is often evaporated by the harsh reality of the sun. It's difficult to straddle the tightrope of joy without falling off at some point. A constitution of endurance safeguards the mind from destructive musings.

Let me say unequivocally that I do not, nor have ever, supported the notion of self-harm as a therapeutic means of emotive release. Dramatic and hyperbolic language aided me in dissipating many a sorrowful feeling of inadequacy and introspective repugnance. Remember, you are loved, and there is always someone who will be more than willing to listen to your stories. Death's circus bears no benefit. The razor, rope, and gun only speak one chthonic language.

Know and love thyself. Be kind to others.

Love has always been the solution. It is the key to the locked heart, a fire to kindle the soul, the gentlest consolation in a cruel world. To walk her serene, lovely pathways allows for the release of pains and overbearing thoughts.

It was on a cold December day that the most beautiful woman serendipitously entered into my life, truly a goddess walking the earth. The wheaten crown of Lada verily rests upon her delightful, graceful head. Leilani, I place this humble work on your altar of peace. May your elegance be immortalized herein, imperishable flower.

I would like to take a brief moment to thank my family, without whose inspiration and support this work would not have been completed.

Always pursue your dreams. To the wonderful team at FriesenPress, it is with extreme appreciation that I offer my sincerest gratitude. An envisioned dream was turned into a tangible reality, and I will be forever grateful.

The final words have been written. Fates, if it is within your will, let this work be blessed.

Michael Finelli

MMXXIV

Part One:
In the Caves
of the Algea

—

Doomed You Are

Boils burst and leak their due
As you succumb to the vileness that is death
Ragged exhalations of unfinished prayers will not help
you now
There is but one way, and easy is it for feet to tread
Invisible eyes of the deity watch satisfied
To feed his lust, you must transcend the veils
To increase his strength, surrender all hope
The mortal world, it is but a memory
Nothing more than a fabled land promised to the gullible
There is no turning back, only death before and after
No respite shall thou find
The fruit from the loins of Cronos and Rhea on his haughty
throne shall avail ye not
Doomed you are, and forever it shall be

Inexorable

There is no way to escape this fate
This maze of languished torment
Every turn compounds confusion
The son of Pasiphae waits in twisting labyrinthian tunnels
Ready to cut the string of order by which one strides
Cloven hooves follow the wanderer in silence
Cretan horns wait to skewer the unprepared at the
opportune moment
Suffer to die, a slow fate, indeed

Titanomachy

The curses of stutterers are uttered
Shrieking ghouls of insanity swirl around my head
Life's crop has failed to produce
Robigus has turned his indignant face against the sorrel dog
The field will wither and die; the invocation falls on deaf ears

The responsibilities of Atlas rest on me
My soul is distal from my corporeal self
In this Titanomachy, the mirror reflects me not
Othrys's misanthropy is pitted against the calmness that
is Olympus
The battle waxes and wanes on a daily basis

Will the Hecatonchires take to the field against such forces
of chaos?
Can the three throwers of rocks placate self-doubt?
Briareos raises a sea storm to oppose malignance
Kottos dissipates insanity with a hundred arms
Gyes gnashes self-hate between fifty heads

The brothers of the hundred-handed ones, the cyclopes
Rally at the behest of Zeus, to fight against their father,
primordial vigour
The forgers of lightning and thunder
The sons of Gaea present bolts to Zeus as a sign of fidelity
The decades-long war will be over soon

The three cyclopes are guarded by the Nymph of Tartarus
Campe of horrendous, chilling, serpentine form
A multiplicity of beastly heads girds her stomach
Bitter venom drips from a lashing scorpion tail
The nails of this formidable drakaina are curved like billhooks

Zeus felled the she-creature with ease
Over the corpse of their jaundiced jailoress do the cyclopes
enthusiastically step
Arges the Thunderer booms in opposition to the fricative
whisperings of Uranus
Steropes the Lightner sears the flesh of detrimental Iapetus,
holder of the west pillar
Brontes the Vivid fights against the rabid reminiscences of
Mnemosyne, memory-titaness

The thunder bolt of Zeus slays tentativeness swiftly
Sorrow's minions reel and flee at the spark of authoritative
electricity, their powers stripped
Courage, the friendly lover of serenity, fills the void
of hesitancy
Under the aegis of love is life conquered
Rhea was wise to substitute the child with the omphalos

The trident of Poseidon pierces antipathy
Vain Medusa covers her face with shame
Many beautifully complexioned individuals are dead inside
The humble are usually gifted caring hearts
Be ever weary of those ugly both externally and internally, a
danger to all

The helmet hath caused invisibility, for Hades
The evasion of fierce blows, it permits
A firm dissociation from scorn and sardonic mistreatment
The bident's prongs of forgiveness and self-compassion are
utilized well
In a confused state of hysteria do titans swat at empty air

The thunderous wrath of Zeus is unparalleled
Unmatched is his tenacity
The overthrower of Chronos claims his rightful throne
The Olympiads are led to consummate glory
Amaltheia cries tears of stellar bliss

Woe

What evil is committed by the wicked hands of humanity
Ample guilt is there for the Furies to dole out retribution
Few on this spinning world are clean of heart
The Sorores Genitae Nocte have unceasing punishments
to inflict

Clothed in hunting boots and sable garments of deepest black
do these goddesses avenge
Slavering snakes slither around supple bodies
Blood-encrusted torches are held aloft
The gates of agitated insanity are opened

Maxillary fangs of serpents inject frothing venom into
malevolent flesh
Alecto's neurotoxic kraits cause paralysis for those who
wished to escape responsibility
Tisiphone's horned vipers deliver hemotoxins, a
vascular shock
Megaera's rattlesnakes extol myotoxic venom, the kiss of
muscle necrosis

Alecto is unceasing in her duty
Abusers of power will she correct
Their towers of pride will she level
Poverty shall enrobe the crooked

Tisiphone redresses murder
Ghosts of the knife-worked and murdered, she calls forth for
the living to see
Kin killers are forced to stare into the eyes of the slain
Culpable hands pull out hair and beat breasts in belated regret

Men butcher for gods, countries, and ideals
This is all a waste, and a supreme one at that
Life is brutal enough without such stupidity
Those who incite such ridiculous notions should be struck
mute, to their chagrin

Equal are humans in their worth and suffering
Folly is it to add suffering to the mortal condition
Misery loves company but has overstayed its welcome
Let it be thrown from the Tarpeian Rock

Humanity has lost its way
Led astray by foreign thoughts
A proud nation cleaved from glory
All for the sake of souls

The grudge-defender Megaera will set to rights
Wrath's putrid essence shall be neutralized
The pervasive need for reckless hate will be sublimated into
productive enterprises
Nihilism evaporated into the ether

Centaurs arrive at a wedding banquet
Amorous glances are cast by the bride at their leader, instead
of her groom
The threshold is never crossed
Much to the ire of intent

As the groom defends his title, he is trampled
The marriage of hoof and skull is consummated
Lobes, cerebellum, and spinal cord are mashed by
the horse-man
A sickening stew of organ's end

This wrong shall be righted
Hydra-dipped arrows will kill this lot
The slayer of Nemean terror rises to the task, commencing his
work with bow and club
An annihilation soon lies beneath the feasting tables; the red
of blood and wine mix

Liars abound
This poisonous cup is passed betwixt friend and foe alike
Marriage beds lie empty as heartbroken sighs are ushered
onto an empty wind
Whilst still alive, deceivers dig until they are six feet deep

Self-serving swine revel in egotistical acts
They care not for the betterment of the world
For a brief moment are they praised
Impiety is not suffered lightly

Backbiters and those slothful are whipped on their heels
Sayers and non-doers suffer the same fate
Let word match deed
Let pride be felled by humility, its nemesis

Children die as greedy men lust for gold that will never
be spent
Empty promises are worth not the exhaled, lying breath they
are readily promised upon
Truth is a recommendation for fabricators, never a mainstay
Let their tongues be ripped unceremoniously from
grinning mouths

The genitalia of rapists and abusers are sloppily sliced from
bodies with adamantine blades
Rabid panthers lap up the blood of predators
As confessions of innocence pour forth
From disingenuous mouths

Gamblers have dice pushed through their money-
glossed eyes
Snake eyes, indeed
The wasting of tangible wealth for the promise of gain
The stakes of impoverishment

Oath breakers shall have their contracts nailed to their heads
The agreements shall be hammered in front of their eyes
So that they can read the fine print of fidelity
What is the point of a promise if it is forgotten the moment
after it is spake?

Rapacious ones shall have their hands burned on whatever
they touch
Working for their own material goods is beyond
their comprehension
Let third-degree burns cover their thieving hands
Let the lesson be learned!

Catherine wheels rotate broken limbs of the larcenous
Jejunum freely hangs from revolving bodies, the work of
moufflon-hilted daggers
The cudgel used for robbing now imparts blows to skin
and bone
A fitting end

People walk into a wall when the entrance is clearly visible
How can such overbearing stupidity be mitigated?
Logic is the answer
Unfortunately, everyone is atheistic towards her ways

Let these people be slain on the altar of intelligence
The weakness of the inner mind is a lie
Man is completely in control of both body and spirit
Anything else, the wise don't have time to hear

Eris

Turn away your face as you offer me my sacred animal
For the Unseen Ones preside over all things, their
wrath unending
Follow my staff, for it shall lead you to the lands of the
lower earth
Where the holiest of creatures preside as my lawful take
Cerberus-howls and agony-cries echo like Jove's thunder in
that realm
Across the Styx we shall travel, towards the ever-present
torches of Hecate

Uprooted

A root, disheveled and worn, has better life
The dirt path, trodden by many, has greater understanding of
these parts
Rain, shed from heaven's gates, has all but dried upon a
cracked soul of hope
An eternal silence encapsulates this veil
All hope shall fade, glimmer and fade
Life's once-proud head has been smashed to dust
Blood drools forth from its reared vice
A blade, a blade to cut flesh and spirit alike
Let its piercing flash blind all doubt
Blood-covered faces of the doomed stare in terror at
leering death
The depths of Tartarus engulf the dead in flames of
the wicked

Eyes of Anuraz

You, who art mere debris floating in waters unknown
Disenchanted and disheartened, forever shall you be
Witches gather under a new moon to recite incantations for
your doom
Arise and kiss the skull signet of spectral glory
Eternally you shall be lost in this endless forest, this
sickening, miasmic mist
Herein all who believe shall perish, and all who
perish, believe
Heartfelt ambitions are aborted by wicked rites
Poison shall enter your lungs, drown you in its sweet caress
The eyes of Anuraz have marked you, and you are his

Morte di Fame

Let the bodies of the festering dead be summoned
Forth to feast upon the living
Those of the painted faces snarl
Showing their sharpened teeth, teeth of death
The feast is set, the trap is laid
The banshee's wail heralds the return of the Dark One
And let his praise be felt and heard throughout the land
For none can stand against the eery beckoning of Charon

Raid

The war band of death rove the land
Minds bent on murder and bloodletting
Sweeping down on the idle village, the conflict begins
Peasants run fearfully for shelter as warriors prepare quickly
for the fight
Archers nock deadly shafts
Swirling snow chills the skin to the bone
Furious combat warms warriors to the marrow
The blood of kinsmen has been spilt this infamous day
Bodies of the broken and dead litter the bloodied snow
The village aflame in the distance, the band leaves the land
Gold, slaves, and more, they have stolen from the now dead
Their unspeakable acts shall live forever through eternity
Head thrown back, their leader laughs heartily at death
committed by his hand
Gods of the blood, his men are
Brazen blades are momentarily sheathed, but ever ready
for blood-craft

Victorious Villain

He crosses the waste
Reclaiming lost lands
Those who oppose him
Shall die in the sands
Bar the gate
Prepare the guard
For he brings beasts
To smash the walls hard
Swords and arrows harm him not
Chosen of gods, he shall stand
At his side, witches fight
With fire white and hot
Lay down your sword, O, defeated
Bring forth the wine and gold
The city lies in decimation
From your life, you shall surely be cheated
On a mound of the dead, he raises his flag
A single stroke of his sword has slain many
The strike of the mace cleaved life from body
He has the applause of his royal hag
Into the mists he rides
Sternness spread across his face
Decomposing corpses screech and claw at their psychotic
faces at his approach
Bones rattle in cacophonous fright

The Way to Valhalla

The field of battle lies in wait
Covetous for the coming butchery
Men form up in ranks ten deep
Their armour glittering in the light like Andvari's ring
Horns resound again and again across the lines
An echo of impending death
The order is yelled, and men rush forth
Eager to draw the scarlet from their sworn foes
Swords raised, armies charge into the melee,
Thor's harbingers
Blessed with war-craft, the gifts of rage and fury
From brow to foot are men covered in blood, the libation for
Asgard's hosts
The pathway to the Bifröst is lined with the sliced intestines
of foe-men
Woe to the warrior whose heart is gripped by fear, for the
gates of Valhalla shall open not
Stand firm, and die with bravery as the weapon descends

Horns

The crescent moon doth kiss the hands of the warrior
Who spills the blood of enemies upon ancient soil
The braying of horns has summoned me to battle once more
A wailing so beautifully destructive
I will rush forth to slay my enemies
See their blood stain my sword
For I am a force of sheer malignance and wrath
I shall show no fear amidst the dead and falling
My strikes shalt render men lifeless on the field of war
Victory lies palpable in the iron-rich air
A forlorn hope now for my foes, but one within my grasp
I advance and I slay
My rune-covered blade is thrust hilt-deep
The cold winds from the mountains rush down upon me
Heightening my already-racing senses
My heart beats like a war drum, as I swing corded muscles
Many warriors have fallen before me
A pile of the dead lies behind me
The freshly fallen snow has turned a bright red from soft,
peaceful white
Loki's pain is felt as a serpentine knife penetrates
epidermal defences
As my muscles are frayed by vengeful steel
I know my time will soon end, but I shall not cower like a
vapid fool
In the far-off clouds, I see the halls of Valhalla,
majestically stunning
The Valkyries, in their shining armour, ride towards me
And, as the handmaidens of Odin approach

I let out one last bestial scream that sees my foes scatter
in fear
Soon, I stand over my body, surrounded by a sea of crimson
I have fought, and I have kept my honour
Pride flows through me like a river as gentle hands bear me to
the sky
To the hall of my ancestors
To the hall of the slain I shall go
Until Ragnarök darkens the skies of peace
And all must be destroyed to be created once more
I hear the braying of horns, and I am content

The Cruel Mirror

The left-hand path she walked unaccompanied
Never knowing that she'd cross Cocytus
Too heavy the burden of pain was
Reaching her brink, she knew what to do
She used her favourite knife on horizontally scared arms
To end her own life
Staring into the mirror, the girl studied herself
Sullen eyes and pale features gazed back disturbingly
A tear distantly slid down her cheek
It turned out that this world doesn't belong to the meek
A trembling hand, she traced through her black hair
For this life no longer did she care
The taunts and jeers from others haunted her mind's eye
For years she had let the comments slide by
The words unstoppably reverberated in her ears
Many a time had she lain low to all the leers
Cold steel now bit into her warm flesh
Crimson freely flowed, and she descended into eternal rest

Thin Slice to Deification

The sheer pain of the terror inflicted upon my soul
is paramount
A vein's thin slice to deification
A destructive whirlwind of repugnance
Intellectually castrated by doubt

Worthless Son of a Cur

You're lucky to die by my hand this day
Skull bashed in, brains askew
The whore who birthed you shall suffer again
Stomach lacerated, guts pulled out
Stretched around your neck like a bloody noose
Son of dirt, you shall perish
Abandon the hope of my mercy
Cold steel to the jugular will send crimson spurting
As it cuts deeper, ever deeper
Blackness of the bowels of Hades reaches up to grasp your
trembling form
Die now, and forever regret your choice this fateful day
My wrath knows no bounds, a titan unleashed
This will not end until you lie dead, even then . . .
Red, sheer red, is all I see
Flames of hate consume my blackened heart
Die, and know no peace

Vampire

The vampiric hand of death reaches forth
To snatch life asunder in the darkest of nights
The return of the undead overlord is immanent
Sucking the blood from saint and unrepentant
Man's crimson ichor drips down a ghastly face
The shadow in the night, the unholy terror
From a catacomb of antiquity did this creature arise
For long aeons has it slept undisturbed
The time of bloodletting has arrived
A Samhain wind rustles fallen leaves
As a silent shadow walks slyly between naked trees
Wolves howl at the full moon
As the unexpecting await their doom
Arisen from the freshly left casket of the tomb
The vampire roves for victims' blood, indifferent to aged
or womb
Decrepit or wise, will he lance
With fangs of purest white
The prize, fresh blood
Uncut nails trace supple, virginal flesh
Fetid breath assails the flared nostril
He is the vizier of the ephemeral night
From death's den
Sojourning from rotting fen
Woe to the beast caught at midnight
Trampled a dozen times under silver-shod hooves
As the church bells ring in angelic harmony
The immortal life of a king is ended swiftly
The bane and death knell

Necromancer's Touch

Moves
The coffin moves
Again
Once more birthed to live
Arise
This death that is life

The crypt shall not hinder my rise
A shallow tomb shall they find
Revenge fuels hatred never matched
Again and again, I shall live this torment

The coffin bursts, wood splinters
I am an eternal thing
All time and space shall fall under my undead dominion
Bow to undeath, as youth bows to age

Kiss the rotting ring of hopelessness,
For I am that which brings utter despair to the hearts of
the optimistic
Pound your naked breasts, for there is no way but through me
The eternal king, the necromancer's touch

Succubus

The Succubus's touch is tender but firm
Her battered wings fold around a fool's hopes
Wicked, onyx eyes will never be true
Still, it matters not to the willing
Their dreams are blinded by immediacy and impatience
Intimacy is short and sweet
But soon, eye sockets are hung from hooks and chains in the
cold caverns of hell

The Whispering of Trees

Dark forests at midnight
Massacre of leaves and bone
Souls eviscerated by unsacred hands
Hounds rip the flesh of light
Hooves trample hosts asunder
The vampire's kiss, the Holy Grail

Ritual

A coven of covetous curse-makers gather in forests deep
To earn their keep, to bring eternal sleep

The cleft lip of a diseased god smirks
As in a hazy cloud of perfumed smoke, he lurks

The ghastly face proudly decrees proclamation of blight
The ushering in of plagues and the loss of sight

Sacrifices will be tonight made
To appease the vilest sovereign of shade

Prisoners are impaled on greased, wooden spikes
Strange, dancing familiars will nibble and conduct
many strikes

Anathematic athames cut through flesh and bone
As bodies are laid on cold stone

Until the dawning morn, these witches slay
Grisly remains will cause devout men to pray

Isaac

Isaac's throat was slit at mount's top
The angelic voice told not to replace the boy with a ram
Blood and stone intermingle with sacrificial delight
The only true son, slain by a father's hand
The vultures strip away juvenile flesh
As a corpse rots away in the elements

That sacrifice shall be witnessed by beings on high
Baal witnesses the affront from Mount Saphon
Steadily, a plan begins to form in the god's mind
To Sheol will he venture, to reclaim a child's soul
The son of El shall do this in spite
A fitting revenge is arranged

A screaming soul is shoved back forcefully into sun-spit
skeletal remains
Organs are formed in a duck-shaped hippopotamus-
tusk vessel
Flesh is knitted like precious satin
Eyes of citrine quartz are fashioned by ethereal
Canaanite talons
Hair regrows, a quick harvest
Blood is crafted like dew of the morning

Shambling down Mount Moriah, the reanimated corpse cries
tears of patriarchal blood

Betrayed thoughts drive the child into a frenzy of
maddened dementia
Baal's otherworldly jesting is heard on the wind
Exacerbating the twice-born
Towards the tent of his father-slayer does he wend
A threshing floor, it shall be; the grain of life and straw of
death shall be separated

Abraham awakens suddenly from troubled, prophetic dreams
A sliver of moonlight catches his son's yellow eyes
The blade that cut the filial bond is held aloft in
Ereshkigal light
Sarah is a witness of her womb-born
The marriage bed will be a fertile crescent of blood
The father of nations becomes the antecedent of none

Why Must He Cry?

He came from the sky
He came to die
He came from the sky
Why must he cry?

Why, why, why must he cry?

Over the hills and far away
That's where he came from, so they say
Over the hills and far away
Where will his forgiveness be this day?

Why, why, why must he cry?

He sees the world in shades of grey
No one knows of his true way
He sees the world in shades of grey
But now, he has to pay

Why, why, why must he cry?

Darkened horizons meet his gaze
His life has been such a maze
Darkened horizons meet his gaze
But all in all, it's just a phase

Why, why, why does he cry?

He thought in life he had it made
But death swept down with a blade
He thought in life he had it made
All in life did fade

Why, why, why does he cry?

Past regrets stalk him within
Cold metal presses against the skin
Past regrets stalk him within
No matter what, he could never win

Why, why, why does he cry?

Life fades away like a mist
The reaper has come and kissed
Life fades away like a mist
And all that's left is an empty hiss

Why, why, why does he cry?

Tears fall from the man's eyes
For he dies, he dies
Tears fall from the man's eyes
But that should come as no surprise

Why, why, why does he cry?

The prodigal son, he lived his life
Behind every door was strife
The prodigal son, he lived his life
Now only death shall be his wife

Why does he cry?
It is over
His soul feels no pain
You are damned, child, but it is over

Musings on the Shore of the Styx

Weeping sores cover the undying hosts
All of the hopes of humanity shall diminish like smoke passed
through a clenched fist
Never shall it be caught
The sickle of Saturn shall smite bodies of mankind and
beast alike
The throne room of Hades swells like syphilitic gumma
Stones hurled by giants crush those present in their misery
Hands are raised to the now-empty throne of Jupiter to
no avail
Sanguine-encrusted steel is lowered to the earth in
chthonic honour
An eternal and ethereal balance of life

68 AD

I have lived the life of a god
Ruled Mount Olympus itself from the cradle of civilization
The last Julio-Claudian king of men was I
Thespians shall whisper my reverence for an eternity
Hark, now strikes on my ear the trampling of swift-
footed coursers
Qualis artefix pereo!

The Tears of Pan

Son of Hermes and Penelope
God of shepherds, brook, and tree

Half goat and half man divinity
Beseeched for Arcadia's fecundity

Friend of Dionysus, drinker of wine
The envoy of satyr and Maenads is divine

They now cross the river Alpheios in summer prime
Radiant gods under the sunshine

Spying Syrinx, he became covetous
The nymph ran from love deemed frivolous

Refuting the god's advances solicitous
She was transformed; the pan pipes were felicitous

Marsyas was felled for pride
A challenge the god Apollo couldn't let slide

For the game of the aulos was this faun skinned alive
The winds gently caressed the body until sweet death
did arrive

The faithful tears of Pan
Cascaded unto Arcadian soil and sorrow's clan

Towards Ladon fair where Apollo by Daphne was outran
A morose sight to behold for both spirit and man

A friend killed by the god of light
Pan screamed with anger, causing fright

The pastoral setting was shaken from valley to
mountainous height
Setting sheepherders and wanderers to flight

The ever-vengeful titans planned an assault on lofty Olympus
A face covered with a grimace

Pan unleashed a scream that caused their chymous
To be hurled from their body, limous

The love of nymphs did you pursue
Even gorgeous Selena did you wish upon your cheek, and
close to you

The intercourse of gods will take place until the settling of
primavera's sweet dew
When, to the goddess's surprise, shaggy thighs were exposed
when the blanket was threw

He is now a diminished shadow, languid and weak
Alongside precious Echo, they can still be faintly heard on
distant peak

In aged locales does Crotus still seek
The now-mythic king on Mount Mainalo's peak

Dis Pater

Unleash my wrath upon those who deserve such
The hissing blade resounds over unknown flesh
This foreign realm, this sorrowful bliss
Dis Pater, grant me your woe, for such is needed
Let my feet's noise make men gnash their teeth
All must reach their summer solstice, and fall, ignominious
Such is the law of He who presides over all, the Invisible One
Even the heavens shall scream their death at Ragnarök,
the twilight
The flesh of Hercules descended into such realms of death
Ever shall the mighty be comparable to the commoner at
road's end
This pasture of life, Elysium

Hades

A grim death encroaches upon thee
An abysmal breach that is eternal
The Styx rises from the land of the dead
Diminishing all hope for the living
Cerberus's howls fill the frightful night
In the realm of Hades, you are forever incarcerated
Bound and chained incessantly in the halls of death
Tartarus roars with its titanous anger
Sisyphus pushes his stone of repentance upwards time
and again
The tongues of blasphemers are forever forsaken
The tears of Persephone fall on broken fruit, the womb of
the land
Jagged rocks and unyielding cold mark the way
The way of death, the way of kings
For the underworld, it has no end

Demeter Roves

From Jove's lofty throne
Proud Olympus, where the gifts are grown
Heroes of old, lavished
The fate of mankind weaved
By Fates three
Arachne's web weaves in the wind
For she had sinned

Demeter's tired feet rove the earth
Searching every berth
The crops to wither and fail
Until her daughter she can hail
The desire of Hades's eye
She cannot spy
Chthonic goddess, in death to greet
Who, of the pomegranate, did eat
From the gloominess of her abode
Past the thrice-headed Cerberus, she strode
Back to terrestrial warmth above
Into the arms of her mother's love

I Shall Bring the Storm

You don't know me more than myself
Imbecilic inbreeds flaunting their idiocy effortlessly
I shall smite you with your own selfishness
My chariot of hate shall render flesh
Stand against me, and the storm I shall bring

And the Storm I Shall Descend

Hand raised, I praise my father of war
Before him, I shall lay the skulls of the defeated
My insatiable sword shall taste virgin skin and crave evermore
My horse's breath shall stir the winds of my madness
The stomping of hooves rends stone
Banners declaring my divinity shall be raised
For I descend the storm cloud of my father of war, Mars Ultor

Thrice for the Temple

Dragged before the walls of my temple am I
Thrice for the essence of my broken dreams, thrice for apathy
A beast's claws sink deep into the soft flesh of ennui
Unfathomable are the depths of their lusts, for the well
is deep
A precipice meant to be the ruin of all creation
Skin, blood, and bone are seared by the majesty that is
Sacra Soleris
Beaten to death by Mater Luna
Keres, take me!

Discovery

An expedition uncovers a wonder in exotic lands
The entirety of a city underground, unfamiliar to the annals
of history
Illuminating lanterns unveil Kauket's secrets
Hieroglyphics cover the columns of an immense hypostyle
A forgotten curse is unleashed upon the intruders as they
mercilessly begin to loot

Nehebkau's punishing snake reels to strike
Fang-poison will push thieves to their graves
Petsuchos patiently waits in murky waters
The Nile River shall run red with blood once more
Maahes, the tamer of lions, stirs war-bliss
Apep readily brings discord

The holiest of burial chambers is opened by men gluttonous
for glory
Ka enters an immaculate saprophagous, reuniting body
and spirit
Decomposed hands slowly slide the hefty stone lid sideways
Antiquated linen-wrapped feet shall tread where mourners in
millennia past wept

The reincarnated Pharoh rises from the stone coffin, much to
the fright of the intrepid explorers
A bejewelled, kingly hand raises a Ra-blessed khopesh
to strike

Archeologists and soldiers are cleaved in half
Adventurers clamour over stumbling flesh to escape the
obscure ossuary
As the lanterns fade and extinguish, undead baboons bark
and grunt in the encroaching dimness
Sobek's children leave the breast of the Nile to rend
A lonely boat of searchers manages to depart unscathed
Their lives shall be terminated by a withered, conjuring
tongue of the Old Kingdom
Disturbers of the tomb shall truly acquire their fate!

Part Two:
Narcissus Stares into a Nightmarish Reflection

———

House of the Shade

In I rode
Across the plain
And I said to my horse
"Once more and again"
And there before my eyes, there it stood
As I knew it had, and always would
The big old house, of wood and age
Known to be haunted, as for my wage
I left my horse, ascended the steps
And I heard a noise, right from the depths
But I pressed on, nevertheless
Someone had to clean the mess
The door I opened, the stairs I climbed
Squeal upon squeal; no one would mind
In the room I sat, to the left of the stairs
In the room I sat, with all my wares
A fog rolled in, so the door I locked
All I heard was the ticking of the clock
But I knew the way was indeed blocked
Tick tick tick tock
I fell into slumber, a deep one too
Nothing would have woke me, not even you
But as the clock struck twelve, I opened my eyes
And right before me was no disguise
He was grey as the sky
And I wondered, I wondered why
For at the foot of the bed was a man of shade

Fear cut through me like the sharpest blade
"Who be you?" he asked, without blame
My voice shaking, I told my name
His voice sounded like a hissing snake
His words I could not shake
"Once, I was like you
Through life's dreams, I flew
Till that sad day that I departed
Never to have finished what I started."
Quick as he had come, so was he gone
Until the next eve, until the moon shone
I rose from my dreams, and he was there
The same as always, with a care

"Life is never as it seems," he said, solemn and true
"And what happened to me is destined for you."

A Modern Prometheus

Aimless hands stretch out before blind eyes
Shall the shackles of my soul perish as I wither away?
A modern Prometheus suffers inside me
Even the one who brought enlightenment lies tarnished on
hard soil
His deeds are forgotten, his memory lost to infernal time
Sing, then, of the glory that is captured in discretion
The woe in love, and terror in the heart of man

The Internalized, Introspective Warfare of the Mind's Eye

The heart weeps in solitude
As an oppressive, crushing sentiment takes over
An idealistic, optimistic mind displaced
A life planned but never attained
The aspirations of tranquility flitters past
As I awaken from a dream of peace
The stability of my happiness
Disintegrated into doubt
As malevolent forces whisper incessantly into my ear
This sibilant, unrelenting energy
Attacks my insecurities
The least-defended portion of my mind's fortifications
The walls will not be surged
For the willpower has been found in love's soft arms
The industrious identity
A playful summer rain falls gently on my skin
Bringing with it a profound hope for the future
The mind carefully treads on a tightrope of sanity
To balance is to straddle life and death, pleasure and dismay,
reality and dreams
Vain ambition will avail me not here
A spiritual change occurs suddenly
My heart weeps for the ubiquitous flare of amorous purpose

A Crucified Heart

It is finished
Sink the nails into unwilling flesh
The nails of repugnance, rejection, and renunciation
The veil of depression will be torn on the third day, and every
day afterwards
Henceforth for all eons of man
As love has not come into my life
The stone shan't be rolled away
I will not be resurrected

Prayer

On this day
Let the child pray
For the displacement of fears
For the drying of tears
The fortitude against sneers
And for the strength in coming years

Let him be empowered with the will to live and love
The most sacred gifts sent from above
On peace's delightful, tranquil dove
Granted through the supplication hereof

A Child's Deposition

Queen Mary, please make the asphyxiation brief
Seraphim, move the chair from under my little feet
Christ Jesus, raise me to your splendour
The end is bittersweet
Mama and Papa, hate me not
For I ascend to a room prepared for me
Tears fall onto a cold floor
As wings lift me to heaven's beautiful door

Hopeless

The forest of knives rises ominously from frozen soil
Branches twist and reach from the firmament to the ground
Inescapable are injuries, for the coniferous-like blades
are unforgiving
These woods are named Life, and none can reach trail's end
without blood loss
Sanity disappears as strips of flesh are sliced off by
dazzling carvers

As I run through this forest of blood, this redwood
Branches swing down to inflict further wounds
Insecurities are reflected on the flat of the blades as
they descend
To the tang, do these utensils remind of the failure of well-
intended dreams
Tears intermingle with drawn blood for the ruination of the
concord between mind and body

Drawn ichor leaves a trail behind, the remnants of identity
Quickening the pace only exacerbates suffering
Slowing down leaves ample time for pitiful brooding
No option is there for my bleeding, frozen feet to halt, even
for a second of respite
Torn veins swinging in the whirling snow, the knife's edge
is negotiated

Stone and Water

A millstone is tied around my neck
I am tossed into the oceans of fecklessness
Doomed to sink and drown in my own failures
Circling sharks rend descending flesh
My bones lay on the seabed, wept over by Amphitrite

Lineage

An unwarranted departure transpires from maternal presence
to paternal abhorrence
The abuse of a child, it brings
The death of innocence
The haunting of a once-serene mind
The maiming of peaceful sighs
Angelic hands console not her pain
The vile acts of a man now dead live still vividly in her brain

Emotive Feelings

Why do I feel this way?
All torn inside
Face front I'm fine
Trapped in this cage of endless fear
An enemy approaches with an ignoble sneer
Taking away from me all that is dear
Egregious attempts are made to reconcile life's blot
Give it all, give it all you got
No point though, for in the end it's naught
Why do I try?
Why do I care?
It's much too heavy of a burden to bear
Drown in lakes of fire
I am a wolf alone
Cease to exist before I breathe

Locomotive

Ischemic views race through a morbid brain
With the methodical thudding of an infernal train
On tracks comprised of lacerated bodies
The Death of Dreams, driven by steam
Lurches forth over a xeric landscape

Winds of Hate

Strip away my flesh
For I am naught but bone and thought
Thrown into the whirlwind of misery
The old self is slain at day's end
Only to be raised on awakening from fevered nightmares
of disillusionment
To the tomb of the Great One, I wander
Solitude my only companion
Falling stars destroy my hopes
The asylum of ill-begotten dreams is my lot in life
A pillar of salt, for all the good intentions

I Loathe Myself

A simple fact for a wasted life
Let my soul burn in the fires of regret
Let memories of me fade into disturbed slumber
Let my body decay into nothingness, for nothingness is me
A ruined life cannot be mended though some would
say otherwise
A shadowed existence is all that I can hope for
That, and the constant sting of vexation
The heavy, acidic rain of life falls bitterly on my flesh
A reminder that my aspirations fall onto barren soil

Turning

When will I be loved again?
Truly loved for being myself
Not what others want me to be?

Will love ever find me again?
Me, who am so far removed from its grace?
A wretched soul full of morosity

The greatest emotion of all evades me
Consciously denying me what I seek
Peace is gone, replaced by anxiety and fear

As the stars are far and distant from me
So too is the reverence of love I once had
A cold winter wind clutches my soul

Long have I stared at the sun's rising
Hoping the new day would bring deliverance
But the hope soon evaporates
And the grim wheel of life turns

It turns

Wasted Life

Utterly futile and insipid
I disgust those near me
For I am unwanted flesh
I blame them not
For the hatred of self is a familiar sting to my spirit
Alone in this life
I wait for the everlasting grave
With none to call a friend
The joys of life are fruitless
A knife in the night would gladly be embraced by my soul
For I am of no more worth than the mud on the ground
Tears of madness I cry under the iridescent sky
But life continues on with its wicked ways

A Solitary, Mountainous Climb

My soul, O, my sweet soul

The mountain path that has led us onwards twists to

inhibit movement

A sickened star hangs over Bethlehem

All lust shall go unpunished, impregnable in the mind's eye

Though I reach out for the hand that was loving, I touch only

the emptiness that is life

All is to be this way, in time

Time slithers, a scythe in the tall grass

Today shall be the same as the rest, evil residing in the heart

of man

Ponderance under a Grey Sky

Grey clouds roll

As rain lashes an ever-wearied soul

Feelings of inadequacy abound

As leaves are aimlessly blown around

A contemplative mind is at work

Attempting to gaze into love's pure eyes through hazy murk

The cold wind cuts deeper than doubt

As I ponder life's drought

The field is all but dead

As rain falls on my sorrowful head

Thunder booms in the distance

As, with a persistence, I dwell on matters of existence

Remorse fills my heart with a sickening premonition

As I strive for a sliver of tangible frisson

Thoughtful Thoroughfare

The road to ruin is vast and paved
All those who walk its crooked way are already enslaved
And you, my love, stride upon the edge of a knife
Destined to become one who is lured

What are we supposed to do?
Your lies have always been see-through
The shadow of a ghost, you now are
Distant are you, distant and obscured

Maelstrom of Fear

Plunged into a maelstrom of fear and fury, we collectively
arise to greet the dawn
Let its pale luminescence burn our flesh
A fitting sacrifice for the eternal burden
Forever shall the world abide this weight, this mountainous
portent of doom
Bloody evisceration awaits the fool-hearted who
seeks recompense
Necromantic rites to summon forth hope from a third-
day tomb
Resurrection or restitution, it will avail ye not!

Unyielding Force

Relentless wind howls across broken flesh
A feeling of utter apprehension and dismay
What worth is there in a life of anguish
A life filled with bitterness and regret?
Failure is my only option and naught else
What good has been done by my hands?
I, who am damned to madness and saddened thoughts
Shall walk the earth in an eternal lament
I, who am worthless and forgotten, shall live to die
My memory shall fade with my body
Hung from a noose of child's tears

Relationship

This pain
It's enough to maim
Sick of all the lies
And all the whys
Fool me once, shame on me
Never what it was meant to be
Fool me twice, shame on you
For making me feel so blue
My hopes still live
I've got so much to give
Was hoping for more
Instead, I get mental gore

Disenfranchised

I have no voice
Though I can still talk
I have no thoughts
Though I can still think
My actions are but mere movements
Serving no purpose
With no soul to lose
My life ends in desolation
A true wretch am I
And death shall be my prize for life

Only Then

Let the razors of undeniable cruelty cut into my flesh
For I have no use for its mortal connection to this
fallen world
Let the lashing winds of the cold winter morn degrade
my soul
For I am but a snake's shadow compared to my past
The zest for life that once filled me like an unquenchable fire
Has now but all been doused
What am I then but useless thought and passion?
The human condition is one of utter despair
What shall become of me, me who is so depraved of life?
The wolves of the northern frosts howl at an empty moon
They care not that their efforts all lie in vain
Dammed and forgotten am I, who art of mortal build
Soon, the distant waters shall cleanse me of all impurities
Only then shall I be truly free to walk in peace of the
summer pastures

Crags

All insecurities of life fade when I am with you
All anxiety is but a dream of the past
Dreaded fear leaves me like winter departs from spring
The coldness of my dissonance gone away for a time
The mountains of hope rise before me now, but ever are they
far away and impossible to reach
Any desire to reach their blessed peaks is worthless
The road towards them is littered with the remains of those
gone before
Shells of ancient imagination, now cursed as evil
But approach the mountain range, I will try
I am compelled on by the music of pipes, faint and cold
The sound soon fades, and I am alone in a world of darkness
once more

The Point

What's the point of living
If all that happens is bad?
We're little more than simple beasts
With lives increasingly more sad
Feelings of despair assail me
Confusion envelopes me
Darker, ever darker
Blind, but still can see
Live your life so you can rot
Work like a slave till you die
Just can't live with what you got
Never falter, never cry
Beliefs attempt, but avail me not
Beings you seek that can't be sought
How many wars? How many fought?
And still peace is a fantasy thought
Seasons change from new to old
Wait for your life to unfold
Who knows where it may lead
Personal hate or good of seed

What's the point?

Hideaway Me

Split me in two
Swallow me whole
Ingest my thoughts
Crush the stars of my hope

Run me through with your sword of scorn
Bitterness festers in the wounded flesh
Unhealed, I shall fade into the Misted One
Till all that remains pure has become decrepit

Float in the sky
Feel the wind
Taste the moon
Shelter the sun

Coil your vices around me
Drown me in your inequity
Water to the neck of the unbeliever
Anger crushing the skull of reason

Red moon 'neath my eyes
Introvert, the soul
Race to the end of the path
Mazes of rendering torment

Bullet from the weapon
Fire under the pyre
Leash for the unprepared
Rope for the ready

Serpentine Constriction
of a Broken Heart

The Python of Delphi crawls silently across
untamed landscapes
The silent slitherer stalks unmindful victims
Slitted pupils scan for signs of movement
A draconian tongue flickers incessantly in the midday sun

This prophetic python ponders proudly from his stone perch
Many a human's broken heart has been consumed by aged
serpentine intestines
Hope lost to blackened maws
Joys defeated by persistent pessimism

A saddened man walks past the stony outcrop where the
beast lies waiting
A fragmented heart is the only possession he still holds dear
in this unpleasant world
Pytho opens its mouth to strike
With lightning speed do teeth clamp down on flesh

How was this victim selected?
A throng of jovial individuals walked past at the same time as
the sad man
Dejection was thus the target for the coiled one
The belladonna heartbeat was easy for the snake to detect

In a purple field of perennial hyacinths does the constriction
take place
The brutal breaking of bones in a bonny setting
Enormous muscles tighten against a weakening, annual prey
The guardian of the omphalos compresses until
enucleation occurs

The dying man calls out to Apollo
The deity of artistic splendour hears the precious pleading
Mercy grips the son of Leto, as he places the Daphne-inspired
laurel wreath upon a wise brow
Trumpeting calls resonate throughout Olympus, as a
departure occurs on the swan chariot

The god of light now pits his strength against dragon's might
Therapeutic love against infected, false forewarnings
Intimacy evades unthinking, brutal force
Wisdom supplants self-propelled folly

Apollo's gilded shafts puncture scutes effortlessly
The persecutor of Leto dies with cyclopean-forged shots to
trachea, lung, and labial scales
Vertebrae are shattered, as a fountain of ectothermic blood
spurts forth
Gaia's son shall be remembered with the Pythian Games

Reaching forth to his devotee
The broken body miraculously heals
All griefs are absconded, as a voracious happiness fills a once
distraught heart
The man springs forth to rejoin humanity's fair dance

Oizys

Within mist-laden, dreary caves
Brains are boiled in a cauldron
Stirred by enthusiastic hands
The daughter of Nyx and Erebos carries out her work
in quietude

Dreams bubble in the iron vessel
Hopeful yearnings are reduced
The stock of mental distress is now uncorked and added
in full
Manic lunacy intensifies the flavour

Erchitu

A guilty man's body is transformed twelve times a year
This bestial alteration takes place on nights of the full moon
Into a were-bull does he transmute; hands become hooves at
night's birth
A grievous fault was committed; the wages of past
transgressions are not forgotten by otherworldly adjudicators
A brilliantly white ox roams the island of Sardinia
The purity of the fur sardonically contrasts with evil
deeds committed
Twin candles are skewered onto silver-shod horns
The shadows of towering tapers flicker on the sides of
remote houses
Petite demons prod this sorrowful beast onwards with
skewers dipped into the furnaces of Hell itself
Laughing at the belaying of the bovine creature
Bellowing thrice outside of a threshold publicises a
wicked portent
The master of the house shall be a slave to the grave in a single
year's time
This blame-curse shall be unceasing
Until the infernally lit candles are extinguished with a single
breath by a fearless individual
Or both of the silver-shod horns are sliced off with a
single strike
Brave and strong shall be the only saviour of this wretch's
afflicted life

In this Mediterranean clime, is there none near Oristano's
west coast that will rise to the challenge?
Is there a valiant soul who ventures out in the brisk night air
around Cagliari?
Or a warrior-hearted man near Olbia?

Scultone

In Sardinia fair
Was a monster's lair
Saint Peter wrestled power from its fetid jaws
And threw the beast straight into Hell's maws
Herein lies the yarn

Peter was born in Bethsaida
Near Galilee's messianic shores a fisherman was beckoned to
become a fisher of men
Andrew's brother will become the rock of the church at the
appointed time
To evangelize nations
Christianity's rising star shall be followed far and wide
To the distant isle of Sardinia does the first witness to the Son
of the Living God go
The Tyrrhenian Sea is sailed
To bring peace to troubled people
Aid to the unfortunate
Salvation to the destitute
Hope to the downtrodden

A heinous monster dwells on the island's eastern coast
A winged serpent this basilisk is
On barren plateaus does this fell creature reside
The terrorizer of Golgo is unmatched
Demanding the sacrifice of nubile, virginal flesh on a
monthly basis

Frightened villagers obey without question, for the purpose
of halting total wrath
In the interim this serpentine king uncaringly sallies forth
with wicked claws a foot long
To slay men and sheep
Victims are petrified with a single glance

Setting foot in Baunei, in Nuoro's province
Is the fate and fortune of the island indubitably changed
A village rushes forth to meet the newcomer
In their midst is a woman most chaste
Her young life comes under the protection of
divine providence
She informs the saint of the great misfortune to befall her
For she is to be sacrificed this very day
Her parents implore for aid
Hearing these beseeching cries, the basilisk laughs now in
merry content
Its serpentine eyes stare down at the villagers
A claw is heard rapping a bone against a discarded
skull insolently
The virgin's name is yelled by scaly, nefarious lips
The marriage bed of tooth and innocent flesh is heartlessly
called for

Peter listens with patience, a hand on a troubled chin
Villagers huddle together to converse
A decision is unanimously decided
The demon shall be removed if a church is built
and consecrated

Ascending swiftly, is the serpent grasped by the tail
Wicked writhing and gnashing of squalid teeth aid not
this reptile
Talons leave not a scratch on repentant skin
Profound words taught by the King of the Universe to the
earliest pope forces this wicked draconian giant to kneel, to
eat dust
Peter sees nailed hands supplement his own
A laugh erupts from his chest, much to the consternation of
the dragon
Death is a worthless rag in the hands of the Lord
The heavy beast is smashed against stony plateau twice; the
earth splits open
The third blow breaches the bowels of the earth
Su Sterru is formed, a cave near bottomless
A wingless flight occurs
As the behemoth falls into the pit prepared for Satan's hosts
Caverns deep still remain to this day

In jubilation do the people of Golgo gather around Peter
A crown of myrtle is placed on his head by the
indebted virgin
A sad memory flashes in his mind of the high priest's
courtyard, of the crown of thorns
Thrice was God denied by his follower's sinful mouth
Three times did he disown the Transfigured One, to weep
bitterly at Christ's forgiving gaze
His spirit was strong, but the flesh was weak
Peacefully and gently does the apostle refute this
empty praise

A man is a man, at day's end
The grave's groan was escaped by Mary's Holy Son

As agreed, a church was built near the cave
Masses are still performed in honour of the
sacred deliverance
Amen!

A Good Life

One often wonders what makes a good life
Is it the deeds we do or perhaps the lifestyles we chose?
Is it based solely on our actions towards our fellow man?
The standard for the measurement, like many things, varies
per person

Our chosen actions in life directly affect those we hold in
our hearts
Though we forget this on a regular basis, it is so and is vital to
the joy of living
A single action can help or hinder many
Ever cautious should one be of the impact of their choices
in life

Regret is an unwanted companion upon the road of life
It darkens the soul and damages the mind
Though the future can be changed, the past cannot
The feeling is a heavy burden to tolerate

The Kissed Shackle

Here I am
Nothing to hide
Bare before you

I place my joys
However small they be
On your altar of cruelty

I'll take the punishment
I'll take the whip
Nothing compares to your iron grip

Soul on fire
Soul of ice
I am yours to do with, in vice

Free, but in chains
You're my love
You're my bane

Rejection

She rejects me with the kindest of words
Gently pushing my hands away from hers
My love is guided away from her heart
Directed to the arid desert of depression to die alone in the
sands of consternation
Such a lofty woman, I could never garner with my love, truly
She is so far out of my league, out of this cosmic galaxy
An alabaster hand is gently kissed, and life goes on its
separate ways
These separate roads will never intersect
No ramp to her highway shall ever be found
I wanted to immortalize her
That foolish reverie has left me in a fevered dream of despair,
staring at my own failures face-to-face
This slippery pit of dismay shall never be escaped
Jacob's Ladder has been lifted beyond my reach
Celestial blessings are now a faint echo
Who would rescue such a bestial cretin such as myself?
It was always a bold hope that anything would surmount
from this effort
Alone I stand, staring into a cold but realistic mirror of my
suffering reflection
Narcissus stares into a pool of nightmarish likenesses before
being pulled under by Vodyanoy
Heart, let us attempt a recovery
It feels like the entirety of the world is crashing down on me
Rash was I to ferment theses dreams inside my
imbecilic heart

The fragmented fictions of a passionate mind
My cheeks are now dry, as I have not a single tear more to cry
In solitude, am I destined to wander and die?
With a full understanding do I appreciate this woman
I wish her a long and wonderful life
Let all graces and bounty be gifted to her
As I wander blindly through this endless fog, seeking solace
in obscure places, far from the empyrean

When Gods Are Fools

When gods are fools
And men are blind
When the path lies crooked
There shall ye find
A glimmer of hope
In the desert of time

The Bridge and the Darkened Forest

Between a bridge and a darkened forest, I stand
Should I proceed forward, into the unknown, or press back,
into the darkness?
That which is unknown may yet still be a danger, some
would say
Going back could be just as dangerous, though
Taking a deep breath, I begin to cross the bridge
The waters swirling under my feet shimmers in the starlight
Life is strange, in its own ways
I stare up at a laughing, content moon
So too am I content, like the face in the sky
A soft breeze caresses my skin, heightening my senses
I feel so rejuvenated from the night air
I have crossed the bridge and now am in a land of light
I walk with a spring in my step, taking in my surroundings
A brilliant sun shines down upon my face, warming me
I am glad for its company this day
A giant tree, in the near distant, rises from the
warmed ground
I journey to it, sitting under its shade
The seasons change, but still I sit
Summer to fall, fall to winter, then to spring, and once more
back to where I was
Every star seems to shimmer before my eyes
I reach out into the bright heavens, my spirit soaring
I am glad I crossed the bridge

My soul is free once more
An eagle soaring over the celestial bodies
I am home
The darkened forest has been left far behind

Purification

May water pass through my hands
A cyclone of which compares not to my heart's delight
An unparallel dream, the likes of which are never seen
Relinquished power, the throne undeterred
Let the torrent through the stygian light of my passion
Let not the poison of my dreams slay an early heart

Gardener

Sweet is the rose that kisses valiantly the sun
How I long for the feeling of love like I once did
But, alas, my dreams are ill-dreamt

The rush of excitement that was common in now obsolete
It is a memory of my past, distant and forlorn
A ship lost aimlessly at sea

The eternal happiness that once I had has faded
Lo, the work of a gardener's hand has seen to that fact
The work of life is now all but an estranged motion

Sitting behind wet windows panes, I gaze out at the landscape
It is so lush, brimming with life and exuberance
It reminds me of my days as a child running under an
open sky

But now the sky, ever clouded, frowns down upon this man
The earth moans liturgies, for even now an age comes to
an end
I know what the outcome of the great event must be

How long has it been since I last held your hand, my love?
Even mere moments away from you felt like a
painful existence
It has been years, my dearest love, and an eternity

But, a smile touches my face, even to this day
For, I know that, through the cloud and rain, I still see
your face
Smiling more brightly than the sun ever could master

Soon, love, we will be together
I feel the time approaching like a welcomed celebration
We shall run together through hidden gardens like we
once did

With open arms, I warmly embrace this destiny
My legacy shall tell of a loving man with a generous heart
What else can one ask for?

Breathing deeply, I exhale for the last time
I close my eyes, for I have lived a good life
Departing this world, I am at peace

I now see your figure once more, my darling
Truly, you have never looked so beautiful, clad in white
You are just as I remembered, and still blossom in beauty
do you

Your embrace I have wished for the longest time
In that single moment, all of my life's joys seem to spring forth
Arm in arm, we leave for the misty-clad mountains of wonder

Part Three:
Venus Born from
Blood and Foam

———

The Fatal Hunting Trip of Adonis

Adonis was gored to death for love
By hoof and tusk, felled by Mars afoul
The god of war, jealous of a mortal man
Disguised as a boar, was innocent blood shed
For half a year, Adonis could ascend from the stygian realm
of Hades
The tears of Venus bought clemency from the
gods themselves
Vitriolic hate conquered by love's paramour

Carissima

Her eyes are reminiscent of the unfurling of war standards
The gladius's final thrust on a defeated enemy
Victory of civility over barbarism
Caligae marching triumphantly through the streets of
sacred Roma
The strike of the splintering sword against the strong scutum
Arrows bouncing harmlessly off galea
Sunshine glimmering on silver phalera
The presentation of the corona graminea
The retreat of the Hannibal's elephantine cohort from Italia
The crushing of his armies at Zama
A cornu resounding over broken Iberian carnyx
Aetos Dios blinding the Celtic boar
The frenzied wine-dance of the Bacchae
The shrill aulos at dusk in a poet's dream
Sprinting lovers on the Apian Way
Ave!

Dismissed

Eyes meet in a sea of strangers
A romance is instantly kindled
Hearts begin to beat in singular, harmonious rhythm

A marriage is arranged
For two to become one
The other's equal and love's servant

As the bride walks down the aisle, a poor man in rags
approaches the end of the pew she is striding by
He bows low, voicing his love for this woman
A presentation of a twine ring is held aloft by shaking hands
of supplication

The bride walks past without a second of hesitation
The man's words fall on deaf ears
She loyally looks to her groom standing by the priest

Another man approaches from a pew in the middle of
the church
He is arrayed in fine cloth; a handsome smile covers his face
as a ring of silver is presented
Words of praise are deceptively spoken

The bride still pays no attention, and continues to walk
the aisle
Her eyes are solely focused on her soon-to-be-husband
Tears of joy begin to slide down an expectant cheek

Near the front of the church, a striking man of affluence calls
out to the bride
Immense wealth is hoisted as a gift of love
A smile more endearing than her groom's forms on a
chiseled face

The bride falters for a moment
Her gaze is split between these two men, the husband and
the stranger
An unbreakable bond is tested briefly, its tensile strength
surpassed and shattered in seconds

For her fiancé is an upright man, caring and true
He is wealthier than the poor man, and more honest than the
finely-clothed suitor
But poorer and less appealing than the rich man

Tears fall from his face as his bride halts in her path to speak
to the rich man
Hopes that soared on bird's highest wings come
crashing downwards
Slain by a foul hunter

The bride makes a conscious decision
Her groom is abandoned at the altar
For wealth and empty promises

The diamond ring falls on the floor
And with it, the groom and sacred vows
Loneliness shall consummate his days

The man returns homeward, greatly perturbed
Sleep evades his mind's peace
Exercised of all joy as a spiritual cancer metastasizes his soul

A lesson has been learned through the pain and humiliation
A bitter truth revealed to a trusting heart
Loyalty is scarce and fleeting

In the grave shall money rot
Useless to dead, decaying flesh
The deeds in this life are all that matter

Reinvigorated

The funeral shroud of love lost
Is now thrown off in favour of a reawakened aim
Of utmost, earnest resolve
A moment of hesitation can lead to regret
Love's sorrows encapsulated in deep, pensive thought
Living in the space between love and peace
The veil is lifted

Damascene

She converted me like Saul on the road to Damascus
Her love is a blinding light that burns my soul with
its strength
A voice booming from the heavens, and yet so tender as a
summer's caress, assails my ears
The lips of love hath spoken just and fair words to my
rejoicing self
Let the crystalline tears of my engorged happiness fall upon
the ground
Let the earth be fertilized with my hopes
Tilled earth shall provide a beauteous yield

Poem for a Girl

Life, with its mysterious ways
Has got me lost in love's haze
To try and find the way out of this maze
I'd be contemplating for days
From nowhere you came
Life after was never the same
Love is the aim
To start a kindling flame
What is the purpose of this life?
This planet is in constant strife
Please don't turn the knife
On a heart, full of love rife

Infatuation

She reminds me of a string of lights on a warm summer night

A mind at ease

An ethereal calmness

An alabaster jar full of precious oil

The transcending of life itself into interstellar, cosmic
tapestries of orbed planets

A never-ending canzone d'amore

Snowflakes fall onto a wind-kissed landscape of
earthen delights

All vibrancy is absorbed by her brilliance

Devotion

The light shines on her beautiful body
How could a lowly man such as me be able to stay in
such intensity?
It illuminates my very being into a frenzy of animated dancing
The imaginings of a divine design reside in me
The child's extreme love and fascination for the autumnal fair
does it instill in me, at every sight
Her smile is time itself, and I wish to reside with the stars
Eternity emanates from her presence
The swirling snow at the solstice cold is her love letter
A tenderness scare seen assists her daily rove

Running Words

My love is like an emphysema marathon
It always falls short, breathless
Staring in wonderment at the finish line
Words will never be able to accurately capture
her exquisiteness
Truly, this woman is sculpted from supernatural marble
Formed with ethereal elements of everlasting elegance

Gothic

Black lipstick leaves an indelible mark
Her raven's heart emanates the cool October breeze with
every beat
Green hair spectrally floats, a reaper's kiss
Knee-high boots trudge through a pumpkin patch

She stands at the cemetery gates like Atropos
Prepared to cut the weft of my life without a second
of hesitation
Her mind in unalterable
The Mount of Saturn rises jokingly

The rows of tombstones delight her
As she nonchalantly walks through a field of aged death
A brown recluse spider descends from the portico of
a mausoleum
The silken art of the necrotizing fasciitis-bringer inspires
dreams of decaying beauty

Pixies float in her sclerae, bewitching me with
their enchantment
By candlelight does she summon the most charming
of moods
The evocation to Sallos has been heard
The duke's crocodile keeps false love at bay

Billowing mist departs to reveal the gates to her lodgings
A warm, purring black cat jumps into my arms as I approach
Her haunted house is exercised
Only to be reinhabited by phantoms once more the
next night

Skeletons in her closet dance a cabaret
In time to the changing of her seasons
At the new moon doth she rid herself of negativity
And at full, wishes for the fulfillment of deeply
inspired dreams

Autumnal Breeze

The willing heart is stirred
Into a deep musing of love's fine art
Mysterious and yet tangible in true form
It flies on wings above hatred's vitriolic scorn

From where does this mystery originate?
Philosophers can debate
On the flower that will gestate
For few in true form will it precipitate

A chthonic sigh from Hades is heard upon fields of flowers
Persephone's fine form wandered unaware of his powers
Demeter's harvest will wane in dedication
Until Zeus on high booms his proclamation

Cupid's fair dart
Inciting an affectionate heart
Son of Venus, releaser of the white dove
Let the earth revel in the yield of love

Rose Gates of Aphrodite

Girl, oh, girl
Step through the frame and into the flame
Love's desire will emerge
A sweet caress to take away the pain
Her nebulous form travels the cosmos
Scintillant flesh flies between the stars of love and lust
Her heartbeat is a tumultuous whirlwind upon my form
The scent of jasmine on her neck brings the utmost delight to
the senses
Sculpted marble that is flesh joins together in the dance that
expels fright
With heaving breast, she completes the act of purest sweat
A vast traverse of moon-kissed landscape is crossed
The rose gates of Aphrodite are entered
An altar of cleanest stone accepts the purest sacrifices
The night encapsulates the intensity of this
conquering emotion
However robust, it will still fade into the nothingness of time
It will be rekindled from the embers of memory
Love is a thirst that is slaked but never conquered

Venus Herself Reborn from Seafoam

O, Muse, share your profound inspiration
For the writing of the words herein
Dedicated to the most delightful of spirits
Avatar of femininity clothed in the flesh of mere mortals

Man's eye can scarce perceive a fraction of integral
beauty therein
She, the progenitor of Rome
Nymphs play their lyres on the languid shores of Cataraqui
for her every sigh
But who is this mysterious entity divine?

Venus herself reborn from seafoam
On lithe feet making a sojourn
Forth to lands of love and solstice fair
Treading upon Gaia's jubilant earth

She, borne by the scallop shell
Amidst the turquoise Mediterranean Sea
A beauteous form unrivalled
Waited upon by Nereids

She of the most refined qualities
Golden hair adorns a lissom frame of purest marble
Supple hands caress Elysian wheat
In that land untouched by sorrow's malice

Twin doves pull her splendid chariot across a caerulean sky
Named Amo and Fides, they fly effortlessly
Amo, bolstered by authenticity
Fides, unencumbered by falsehoods

Love emanates from her untainted heart
Aided on its course by a Zephyrus wind
West wind, carry her lovely song over hill and valley
To the most willing of hearts

Her beauty graces meadows sweet
Daughter of Uranus, how fine thine loveliness
Asters brighten with purple delight upon your approach
The pomegranate and rose flourish abundantly in the vicinity
of such elegance

By sparkling brook this goddess walks
In the spring of youth's fair countenance
Age will never diminish her beauty
Nor the years detract from the immensity of her perfection

Empathy is her diadem
Compassion, her sceptre
The cosmos rests in a tender hand
This regina of utmost earnestness

Generously blessed are those who act in veracity
Grievous is the heart that is lead astray from her piety
With love does one carry the standard
Amore's signifier

Mankind may hope for a life of longevity
A century, if blessed by the Fates
A single moment in your presence
Is like unto an eternal kiss of time

Venus Felix, bless these words with your loving approval
Reproach not the sincerest of hearts
Verticordia, let not the words die amidst the grave of despair
O, Changer of Hearts!

Leilani

A leap of faith leads to a chance encounter
The most gorgeous of women does this boldness usher in
Verily this woman is unparalleled in beauty
December's bleak chill is thwarted, yielding to the
heart's warming
Leilani, Leilani, Leilani
She truly is a goddess walking verdant earth
The wheaten crown of Lada rests upon her graceful temple
Voluptuous vitality shall not fade from her life
Piercing blue eyes are evocative of the majestic Vistula
Her smile dispels the drought of loneliness
The heart leaps at her kind gaze, the uncorrupted aspirations
for the future
Cascading brown hair falls on Carpathian-chiseled skin
exquisitely refined
This woman dances to the rhythms of life
Dismantling earthly strife
Irreproducible are her divine qualities
Your heavenly flower shall not wither with age, nor the
seasons touch your splendour
I hear you calling from Tkaronto, where trees stand in water
A tantalizing voice enunciating the birth of spring after
winter's cruel and depressive sway
The shifting of emotions takes place; despondency
transmutes into profuse joy
The tender sail of love is unfurled
Shall it lead to the tranquil sea of dreams, or to capsizing in
storms of unrequited unrest?

Acclaiming words from the purest heart will never capture
the immensity of your grace
Leilani, how lovely you are!

About the Author

Michael Finelli started writing from a young age. His interests in history, religion, mythology, and storytelling, along with his personal experiences, inspire his creative work and the poems in *The Tears of Pan*. This is Michael's first book.

He lives in Hamilton, Ontario, Canada. You can follow Michael on Facebook (Michael Finelli – Author) or Instagram (michaelfinelliauthor). His email is michaelfinelliauthor@hotmail.com.

Printed in the USA
CPSIA information can be obtained
at www.ICGtesting.com
LVHW020826290224
773140LV00002B/45